S0-AFM-717

DISCARDED

CH-46 SEA KNIGHTS

BY CARLOS ALVAREZ

™

Are you ready to take it to the extreme?
Torque books thrust you into the action-packed
world of sports, vehicles, and adventure. These books
may include dirt, smoke, fire, and dangerous stunts.
WARNING: read at your own risk.

Library of Congress Cataloging-in-Publication Data

Alvarez, Carlos, 1968-
CH-46 Sea Knights / by Carlos Alvarez.
    p. cm. − (Torque: Military machines)
  Includes bibliographical references and index.
  Summary: "Amazing photography accompanies engaging information about CH-46 Sea Knights.
The combination of high-interest subject matter and light text is intended for students in grades 3
through 7"−Provided by publisher.
  ISBN 978-1-60014-579-7 (hardcover : alk. paper)
  1. Sea Knight (Military transport helicopter)−Juvenile literature. I. Title.
UG1232.T72A45 2011
623.74'65−dc22   2010034496

This edition first published in 2011 by Bellwether Media, Inc.

The images in this book are reproduced through the courtesy of: Ted Carlson/Fotodynamics, p. 20
(small); all other photos courtesy of the Department of Defense.

Printed in the United States of America, North Mankato, MN.
010111   1176

CONTENTS

THE CH-46 SEA KNIGHT IN ACTION

A small group of United States Marines is in an enemy jungle. Enemy forces are closing in on them. The Marines are surrounded and outnumbered. Suddenly, the Marines hear the chop of helicopter blades. Four CH-46 Sea Knights hover over a nearby clearing.

The Sea Knight crews open fire with **machine guns**. The helicopters then land and unload 100 heavily armed Marines. The Marines work together to push the enemy back. The enemy is forced to **retreat**. The Marines continue their **mission** as the Sea Knights rise into the air.

A Sea Knight's engines can lift the helicopter more than 2,000 feet (610 meters) per minute.

MEDIUM-LIFT ASSAULT HELICOPTER

The CH-46 Sea Knight is a medium-lift assault helicopter. It is mainly used to carry U.S. Marines into and out of combat. The Sea Knight is one of the largest helicopters in the U.S. military. Its powerful engines and **rotors** give it a lot of **lift**. This allows it to carry up to 25 Marines or transport up to 5,000 pounds (2,270 kilograms) of cargo.

The U.S. Navy used a version of the Sea Knight until 2004. The Navy's Sea Knight was mainly a search-and-rescue helicopter.

The Sea Knight first entered military
service in 1964. The United States Marine
Corps has used it in every major conflict
since then. The helicopter's ability to
transport troops and supplies played a
large role in the Vietnam War.

WEAPONS
AND FEATURES

The Sea Knight needs plenty of power to safely carry heavy loads. Two T58-GE-16 **turboshaft** engines provide 1,770 horsepower each. The engines are **coupled**. This means that the helicopter can still fly with only one working engine.

The engines power two sets of rotors. The rotors work in **tandem** and spin in opposite directions. This lets the Sea Knight move forward, backward, and sideways.

The U.S. Marine Corps plans to replace the Sea Knight with the V-22 Osprey. The Sea Knight will remain in service until at least 2012.

V-22 Osprey

The Sea Knight needs to protect itself and the Marines it carries. If a Sea Knight is under fire, it can release countermeasures to confuse enemy missiles. The Sea Knight can also fire at the enemy. It has a GAU-15/A .50-caliber machine gun mounted to each door. These guns can shoot up to 750 rounds per minute. The Sea Knight can also be fitted with an M240D machine gun. This gun can fire up to 950 rounds per minute. Both guns provide plenty of support for Marines during missions.

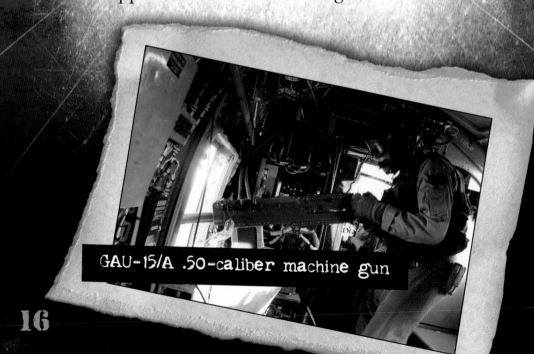

GAU-15/A .50-caliber machine gun

CH-46 SEA KNIGHT
SPECIFICATIONS:

Primary Function: Medium-lift assault
helicopter

Length: 45 feet, 8 inches (13.9 meters)

Height: 16 feet, 8 inches (5.1 meters)

Rotor Diameter: 51 feet (15.5 meters)

Maximum Weight: 24,300 pounds
(11,022 kilograms)

Top Speed: 167 miles (269 kilometers)
per hour

Ceiling: 10,000 feet (3,048 meters)

Engines: Two T58-GE-16 turboshafts

Crew: 4-6

18

CH-46 MISSIONS

The Sea Knight's most common mission is **assault support**. It quickly brings Marines and equipment wherever they are needed on the battlefield. The Sea Knight is also sent on search-and-rescue missions to find lost Marines. It can transport injured Marines to receive medical care.

19

A Sea Knight crew needs to work together to complete missions. A pilot and co-pilot fly the helicopter. A **crew chief** is in charge of the passengers and cargo. A **mechanic** monitors the CH-46's weapons and cargo systems and makes any needed repairs. Two **aerial gunners** can be added to the crew to operate the machine guns on combat missions.

The Sea Knight has been the backbone of Marine transport for many years. Its ability to transport Marines, supplies, and equipment has made it critical to the success of the United States Marine Corps.

GLOSSARY

aerial gunners—crew members who operate the weapons on a Sea Knight

assault support—the role of quickly bringing troops, supplies, and equipment to a combat area

coupled—joined together

crew chief—the member of a Sea Knight crew who is responsible for the cargo and passengers aboard the helicopter

lift—the amount of weight a helicopter can carry

machine guns—automatic weapons that rapidly fire bullets

mechanic—the crew member who operates a Sea Knight's weapons and cargo systems and makes needed repairs

mission—a military task

retreat—to go back to a safer location

rotors—sets of rotating blades that give helicopters lift

tandem—together; the Sea Knight's rotors work in tandem.

turboshaft—a type of engine that produces power by spinning a drive shaft

TO LEARN MORE

AT THE LIBRARY

Alvarez, Carlos. *V-22 Ospreys*. Minneapolis, Minn.: Bellwether Media, 2010.

David, Jack. *United States Marine Corps*. Minneapolis, Minn.: Bellwether Media, 2008.

Von Finn, Denny. *Military Helicopters*. Minneapolis, Minn.: Bellwether Media, 2010.

ON THE WEB

Learning more about military machines is as easy as 1, 2, 3.

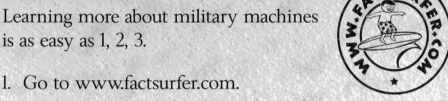

1. Go to www.factsurfer.com.

2. Enter "military machines" into the search box.

3. Click the "Surf" button and you will see a list of related Web sites.

With factsurfer.com, finding more information is just a click away.

INDEX